TAKE HEART

Be Encouraged

Shared by
Kerry Lynn

Take Heart Books

ISBN 978-0-9575065-0-3

Scripture quotations taken from the Amplified Bible, Copyright 1954, 1958, 1962, 1964, 1965, 1987 by The
Lockman Foundation. Used by permission of The Lockman Foundation.
(www.Lockman.org)

Published by Take Heart Books

Printed by The Alpha Xperience, 148 Kings Road, Newbury, RG14 5RG

For you,
Mom and Pop.

Thank you for always loving me unconditionally.
For your constant support and encouragement.
For always standing with me.

Thank You God for blessing me with these beautiful people as my parents,
and for the privilege of sharing our journey together.

And thank you, to all who have encouraged and helped me to grow!

Contents

Take Heart!

To be confident or courageous.

To gain courage.

Give encouragement to.

Hearten.

To give strength, courage or hope.

To inspire with hope, courage or confidence.

To give support.

To stimulate.

"For they all saw Him and were agitated
(troubled and filled with fear and dread).
But immediately He talked with them and said,
Take Heart!
I AM! Stop being alarmed and afraid."
Mark 6:50

Introduction

Many Christians have dramatic stories of huge life style changes from lives of addiction, or abuse, or neglect and rejection, into a totally new way of living. However, mine is not one of those! Nevertheless, it does not make it any less powerful. God works in each of us, wherever we are at! We are all unique, we are all special and we all have a personal journey to walk with Him. Mine began just after I separated from my husband, nearly 5 years ago. I am a 51 year old Mum and I live with my youngest son. My eldest lives with his Dad although is away at university. I have found it a real challenge adjusting, and I have had lots of ups and downs, made good choices, and bad ones!

However, thanks to my beautiful boys, my wonderful loving parents, incredible family, great friends, and my amazing new relationship, I have surprised myself! I am managing to cope, despite my initial fears of thinking that I would not!

How am I doing it?

Well, I have been walking with my awesome saviour, Jesus, and He has radically changed my life... and **still** changing it! We all have our own testimonies, and it is good to share your story with others.

My testimony is that Jesus rescued me from a pit of depression and despair. I had spent years constantly fighting in my own strength to climb out of the pit of darkness I constantly found myself tumbling into. Jesus came down, scooped me up, lifted me out and stood me upon a rock. Light! No more darkness. Then..... He showed me that he had filled in the pit, to re-assure me that I did not need to fear stumbling back in. He showed me a new way to live! Praise Him!

I have been using my time since then, to read the Word, pray, journal, listen to teaching cds and Christian worship music. To watch God TV, spend time with my wonderful, incredible, beautiful family and friends who love me, support me, encourage me, teach and share much with me. I belong to a fantastic church called Lifespring in Reading, who provide encounters and courses to consolidate my faith and equip me. I also meet up every week in a smaller group (cell group), where my amazing cell leader disciples us, loves and encourages us. We all support each other. My confidence is growing. I joined the local Street Pastor organisation over two years ago, which is a great way to reach out, and to meet people. I hope that soon, I will also have my own cell group to disciple.

I am so blessed to have received an understanding, almost as soon as I asked Jesus into my life, that pictures, dreams and co-incidences are some of the ways in which God speaks to us. It has been such an exciting change in my life, and totally goes against what most of us think, prior to being a Christian, that it will be boring!

We can feel fearful of the possible changes that we will have to make when we give our lives to God, but there is no need! No! He gives us the amazing power that enables us to have freedom to live a life that is beyond our wildest dreams, more than we can dare ask, pray or imagine!

God uses our imagination to speak to us, and He has really given me a wonderful revelation about this special place.. The Imagination!

This is where we meet God. It is the 'secret place' of the Most High, where we can talk to Him, hear Him, walk with Him, run with Him, spend as much time as we like with Him. And He is patiently waiting for us there, all the time, every second of every minute of every day.

God soon planted the idea, in my imagination, that I should use the pictures, and words He blesses me with, to encourage others. He told me to create a book, using the images that He has put into my imagination, to bless other new Christians.

So, in this book I have shared some of these. I have tried to find similar images that relate as closely as possible to those that I received from Him. I really hope you enjoy them and find them as encouraging as I do.

How can I hear God?

This is such a common question, especially for those who have just made the exciting decision to invite Jesus into their lives.

One of the most obvious ways is through our **conscience**. Its that check we get in our hearts when we know we are doing something we shouldn't. A small still voice within us that is encouraging us to make right choices.

The Bible reveals God's words. We call it **The Word**. It is not like a normal book, it is a living book. Why? Because the Holy Spirit uses it to get our attention by using different scriptures to leap out at us from the pages. To show us something that is relevant to our lives at that moment, that will help us through it. It's amazing how many times He has done this for me. It is so exciting when you realise God is speaking directly to you! Yes.. The Creator **is** patiently waiting, wanting, to speak to YOU!

Prayer is speaking to Father, and it should feel comfortable, as He loves us so so much, He really does. Don't be afraid, or intimidated, He is so patient, loving, and kind. He has been waiting for you to come to Him for so long. He is not angry, condemning or judgemental. No! He is overjoyed that you are **choosing** to have a relationship with Him.

God can use **music and lyrics** to reach out to touch us, teach us and/or heal us. The same with everything on this earth that He has made. We just need to have our eyes, ears, hearts and minds completely open to receive all that He is showing us.

He is there, ready, all the time. A practical way to explain this, is to think about when we switch on a radio. We can do this any time we choose to and hear the sounds emanate from it. When we decide to switch it off, the radio waves are still there, but we have chosen to disconnect ourselves from it. It's a good way of understanding how we can connect to our Heavenly Father... we can choose to do so at any time!

I also, soon realised, that He could bring pictures into my thoughts. In order to explain things He was trying to share with me, to guide me and teach me. To show me how He loved me **so** much.

It came very easily to me, and I am so thankful as it has proved to be such a blessing. I realise though, that many find this difficult, as well as hearing generally from Him. When you have this in your mind, it can then become a barrier to receiving, which becomes a huge obstacle. Sadly, this can then develop into a mental block that can seem insurmountable. What should be such an enjoyable experience becomes an anxious time, full of disappointment that can involve feelings of confusion, rejection and emotional pain.

Father said to me one day, that He has created a way to communicate with His children that is simple and easy, yet barriers have built up to such an extent it is overpowering their minds. So, if you do struggle at any time, pray and ask God to help you, He will!

Please. Keep on trying... keep believing! Don't ever give up.

It really is a matter of coming to Him, with child like faith, that does not question with the natural mind.

God revealed to me how using our imaginations can be a vital key to a fulfilling, exciting, amazing and fruitful relationship with Him. Our imagination is linked to our mind, and... our heart! We need the connection with all three to spend precious time with Him.

He showed me that when you imagine talking to Him, imagine walking with Him, or sitting with Him... He will come to you, there, in that secret place. It is so exciting, as you can use your imagination to place yourself somewhere, anywhere you want to be, and that is where He will meet you.

A useful way to focus on this, is to journal. To sit quietly, or maybe with some music on low in the background. With your book open, and pen ready, begin to imagine yourself in a favourite place with God, or maybe walking along the beach, or in a beautiful bluebell wood, anywhere that you would find relaxing. Listen, be still. Or ask a question. Or right down a scripture that seems relevant and ponder on it.

You will hear words. They can come from three places. You, the enemy or ... God. If they are **good**, and are in line with **His Word** and **His Will**, then you are hearing from Your Heavenly Father.

As the words come, write quickly, to keep the flow. Yes, you may think that you are making it all up to begin with. But, when you stop and read it back you will be amazed at some of the things you have jotted down! If you believe it, you will receive all that He is trying to teach you, share with you. You will receive His awesome love He has for you in an exciting, unbelievable way. The key is to use your faith and believe it is Him speaking, and then you will receive so much from it.

God desires to speak to us, in order to encourage us to change, and to follow his directions to fulfill His plans that He has for us, to prosper not harm us. It is a two way relationship and a two way conversation.

We may be asking Him for things. However, He will be asking things of us! When we choose to follow His ways, His direction and leading, our lives **will** change... for the good. We do need to be still, and listen and very importantly... **do** as He is guiding and teaching us. He wants the best for us, He has planned the best for us, so when we do as He says, our lives will be blessed, in abundance, in every way. We must be **doers** of the Word, and **doers** of His leading.

Power of the spoken Word

Father has also been showing me how vital it is to speak out His words. It is so powerful. Words are powerful. God's Word is the power to change things, to bring His will here on earth, His kingdom come. If we need healing, find healing scriptures and speak them out regularly, as you would take medicine, and your healing WILL manifest. The same with provision, if you are in a difficult financial situation. Or need guidance for relationships or decisions. God's words are His promises and He never breaks His promise. I appreciate that on occasions doubt can sneak in, so I encourage you to lean on Mark 9:24, "Lord, I believe! (Constantly) help my weakness of faith!"

Whilst compiling this book, Father revealed on many occasions, in different ways, and using a variety of people how important our imagination is. He also showed me that this included speaking OUT His Words.

So, IMAGINATION, PROCLOMATION and MANIFESTATION!

Imagine it,
really picture it clearly, focussing on it in your imagination.
Pray for it,
in the name of Jesus and through the blood of Jesus, and use relevant scriptures to continually speak it out. Thank AND praise Him for it, whilst you are waiting to 'see' it! Keep picturing it in your imagination. Keep choosing to believe. Our God is faithful!
Manifestation of your prayer!
If it all lines up with His WILL, it WILL happen.

Notice, the word WILL. The word has two meanings doesn't it?
Will : inheritance
Will : the power of a conscious action or choice

If we can imagine it, speak it out in faith, receive it in faith even though we cannot YET see it, but continue to stand on that word, then it WILL come to pass. Don't ever give up. Whilst you keep believing He is able to keep working in the situation. When you give up, it disables Him. That is why it says in Hebrews, "Without faith it is impossible to please Him". If He does not seem to be answering a specific prayer, and you are choosing to still believe... then there is a reason. It is not because He is saying no. It is because He is either waiting for the perfect timing, or... He has something even better planned! So, do not get disappointed or disheartened. Choose to keep seeking God, choose to diligently seek His presence... not His presents! He is your Heavenly Father, and loves you and has a great future planned for you.

Do not limit God. For **He is LIMITLESS!** Use your imagination! Don't limit dreams or prayers!

"Now to Him Who, by the power that is at work within us, is able to do super abundantly, far over and above all that we dare ask or think, infinitely beyond our highest prayers, desires, thoughts, hopes or dreams." Ephesians 3:20

Then God astounded me, yet again! It is such an incredible feeling when He gives you an exciting, wonderful revelation! It is one of the best experiences when you know that your Heavenly Father is showing you something fantastic, and He is taking the time to show YOU!

He said the word 'image', as that is what we see in our imaginations isn't it? A picture. An image. Then He said to look at Genesis 1, (verse 26) of my amplified bible.

"God said, Let Us (Father, Son and Holy Spirit) make mankind in Our image, after Our likeness, ..."

Why would He have said, "in Our image, after Our likeness"? Afterall, it is saying the same thing, UNLESS, 'Our image' meant the image they had in **their** imagination! If so, then it makes complete sense, doesn't it?

In the imagination of God, He saw an image of what He wanted man to be. He visualised them, and decided that man would be in their likeness! So, God imagined man, spoke out His words, and then man was created.

And, likewise, when it says in John 5:19,

"So Jesus answered them by saying. I assure you, most solemnly I tell you, the Son is able to do nothing of Himself (of His own accord); but He is able to do only what He sees the Father doing, for whatever the Father does is what the Son does in the same way (in His turn)."

Jesus said He was able to do nothing of Himself, for He needed the Holy Spirit, just as we do.

He was able to do only what He sees His Father doing. In other words He follows what His father does.

He follows (the example of) what His Father does. The example of when God created the earth and man and all the wonderful things on this earth. To imagine, speak it out and see it. It is bringing the 'unseen' (although it is seen in your imagination, but only you and God can see it), to where everyone can see it. From the invisible to the visible. From the supernatural to the natural!

All this that I have shared, may seem PLAINLY obvious to some of you. You may already understand without really having to give it too much thought. It is how we dream big things for ourselves isn't it? We imagine it. So, obviously God did the very same thing when He decided to build His creation. However, I think to explain it, will help many to step into a new relationship with Our Heavenly Father.

When you ask our Heavenly Father for something, pray with the authority and power that you have 'through the blood of Jesus, in the name of Jesus, (saying those actual words aloud as you pray). Pray, believe and receive it IN faith. Believing, that when you have prayed for it, it is on its way. Then begin, and continue, to praise God and thank Him for it. Even if it is still in the 'unseen'.... choose to believe that it is yours! PRAISE! PRAISE! PRAISE!

I have seen some amazing answers to prayer. Here are a couple of wonderful blessings. My Dad was waiting for an operation on his tongue. Due to some previous damage and not so neat stitching, there was a very large swollen lump protruding from the middle. It was so big and uncomfortable for him, making it difficult to eat and talk. He was told it would have to be removed surgically. We prayed for healing, and within two days the lump had disappeared, even the old scar had vanished, just a perfectly smooth tongue! Thank the Lord!

A friend, was informed by her Consultant that she now had one leg shorter than the other, due to illness and operations. We prayed, asking for them both to be the same length as she was enduring pain in her hip because of it. Unfortunately, she fell and needed another operation and it was explained that this would result in the shorter leg becoming even shorter! However, the xray that followed her operation showed that both legs were now, actually the same length! Praise God for His faithfulness!

A young man, suffering from severe back pain, was given the results of an xray which diagnosed that he had Spina bifida occulta. Due to horrendous pain on one occasion, he received prayer. Shortly after, an mri scan was taken to ascertain more detailed information and possible treatment. However, the results revealed there there was no spina bifida occulta! Thank You, Jesus!

Thank each part of the Trinity. For they all play a part! I found it hard to understand the Trinity and how they worked together. Someone suggested, to think of water, it is also ice and steam. All three are one. A useful analogy, although I heard another example. I do not want to seem disrespectful in sharing this, it is just a way that was demonstrated to me about how their combined power works..... as One!

When we order something from the internet, we request it from a company, the credit card is needed for payment, and then the delivery man brings it to us.

We pray to Our Father for something, (whether it be healing, provision, confidence, strength, patience, wisdom, discernment or anything you may need help with), and Jesus precious blood was the payment, and the Holy Spirit brings it to us, from the unseen to the seen.

I hope this simple way explains HOW important The Trinity is to us, how important EACH one is. Without one, nothing can be completed. They are all connected. Imagine 3 people holding hands, each one is connected to the other. Complete unity. Complete power!

Also, we are a three part being aren't we?
Mind
Body
Spirit

The Trinity is a three part being isn't it?
Father
Jesus
Holy Spirit

How to use this book

I wrote this book to share the images and words of wisdom that God has blessed me with, in the hope that they will bless others. I have included scriptures too, as they are relevant to the message God is giving us. Choose a scripture that you are drawn to, write it down, carry it with you and speak it out as often as you can.

I began typing them out and laminating them, cutting into strips and sticking on mirrors, using as bookmarks, attaching to keyrings or hanging in the car, so I could see them every day. Speaking out God's Word is **powerful!**

I also would like to encourage others to take time to be still, listen and hear God speaking to them, through words, or images or both!

So after each image and word I have shared, you will see a list of scriptures, and a page for your quiet time. Ask God to speak to you about them, ask Him, is there anything He wants to show you? Have your pen at the ready! If it is good, if it is 'for you and not against', in line with His will, then choose to

believe that what you hear is Him!

At the bottom of these pages, you will see a scripture (adapted) of who you are in Christ. We need to know, and be reminded regularly, of what it means to have asked Jesus into our lives. Jesus brings freedom, releases bondages and makes us a new person, but we have to renew our minds. Whatever age you are, when you receive salvation, you will need to wash your mind from the way you used to think, to a new way of thinking. It is why we need His Word, running through our minds to counter attack thoughts from our past mindsets, and from the lies, that Satan whispers to us.

Also, if a certain image or scripture is helping you, then keep the book open at that relevant place, so you can be reminded of His words of wisdom and support. These visual reminders are so important, as you walk your new path!

I love you,
believe it and then you can receive it

I was listening to a teaching cd and followed a suggestion to kneel and ask God to show me how much He loved me.
He really does love us! He loves each and everyone of us unconditionally with an everlasting love. He loves us!

I did as suggested. I heard Him!
God told me to go to the patio doors and look up at the sky.

Amazing! I had never seen such a beautiful array of small individual rounded fluffy clouds. Supernaturally they began to move to form letters. A letter 'I', then a heart shaped cloud, and then a 'U'. (I love you.) Then others formed a hand, as though it was reaching out towards me. Like a hand that rests upon you if someone is praying for you. Then a hole formed in the hand!

I gasped..."I'm making this up, this is not really happening."

God instantly responded. "If you believe what you are seeing, and that it is from Me, then you will receive what it is saying to you. You will receive the love. It's like everything I try to show and share with you – if you choose to believe it then you will receive it!"

I chose to believe it, thank You Heavenly Father. I love You, too.

Scripture:

"Truly, I tell you, whoever says to this mountain, be lifted up and thrown into the sea! And does not doubt at all in his heart but believes that what he says will take place, it will be done for him."

Mark 11:23

"Such hope never disappoints or deludes or shames us, for God's love has been poured out in our hearts through the Holy Spirit Who has been given to us."

Romans 5:5

"We love Him, because He first loved us."

1 John 4:19

"We know (understand, recognise, am conscious of, by observation and by experience) and believe (adhere to and put faith in and rely on) the love God cherishes for us. God is love, and he who dwells and continues in love dwells and continues in God and God dwells and continues in him."

1 John 4:16

"I will be glad and rejoice in Your mercy and steadfast love, because You have seen my affliction, You have taken note of my life's distresses."

Psalm 31:7

"Unto You, O my Strength, I will sing praises; for God is my Defence, my Fortress, and High Tower, the God Who shows me mercy and steadfast love."   Psalm 59:8

Why not use this opportunity to ask God to show you, tell you, how much He loves you.

…...

…...

…...

…...

…...

…...

…...

…...

…...

…...

…...

…...

"I am in Christ, and Christ is in me." John 14:20

Let go and let God

I was sat quietly, trying to make a very difficult decision. It was a very important one and I didn't want to get it wrong, so I asked God what I should do. He gave me a great picture!

A cliff, with an old bare tree perched near to the edge.
Its spindly branches hanging over the side.
I saw myself gripping tightly to one of them, dangling in mid air.

He then changed the scene …
I had lost my grip, and as I did so a huge hand immediately appeared under me, ready to catch me, keeping me from any harm!

And I heard...

"Let go and let God."

Scriptures

"For I know the thoughts and plans that I have for you, says the Lord, thoughts and plans for welfare and peace and not for evil, to give you hope..."

Jeremiah 29:11

"For God so greatly loved and dearly prized the world that He (even) gave up His only begotten (unique) Son, so that whoever believes in (trusts in, clings to, relies on) Him shall not perish (come to destruction, be lost) but have eternal (everlasting) life."

John 3:16

"For I the Lord your God hold your right hand; I am the Lord, Who says to you, Fear not; I will help you!"

Isaiah 41:13

"For You, Lord, will bless the (uncompromisingly) righteous (him who is upright and in right standing with You); as with a shield You will surround me with goodwill (pleasure and favour)."

Psalm 5:12

"May blessing (praise, laudation, and eulogy) be to the God and Father of our Lord Jesus Christ (the Messiah) Who has blessed us in Christ with every spiritual (given by the Holy Spirit) blessing in the heavenly realm."

Ephesians 1:3

Did anything resonate in you as you looked at the picture, or the words? Maybe a scripture jumped out at you. Go ahead, ask God something that is on your heart about your future, your life.

…...

…...

…...

…...

…...

…...

…...

…...

…...

…...

…...

…...

"The truth has set me free." John 8:31

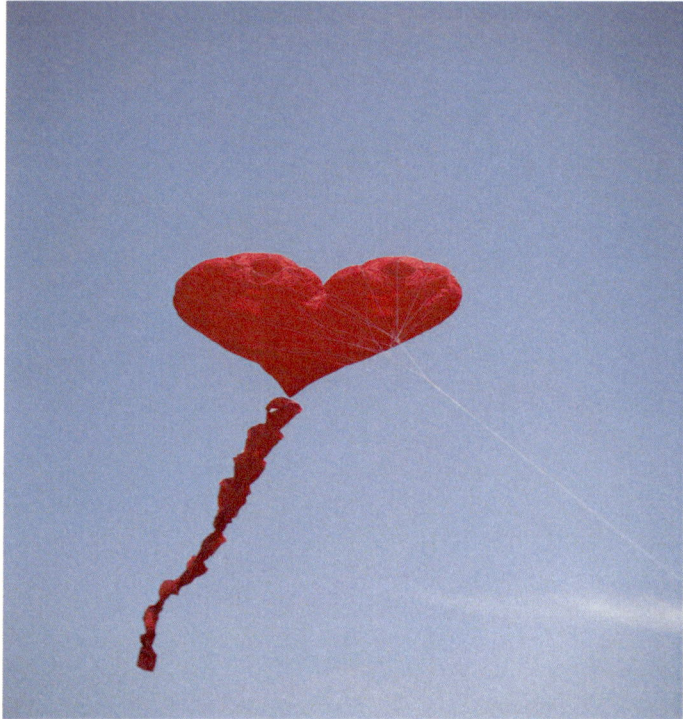

Untangle the kite strings, you'll rise higher

A beautiful kite glides majestically in the bright blue sky. However, it is being restricted from flying freely as the string is tangled up amongst the branches of an old, gnarled dead tree.

Father explained. You are like that kite suspended in the air, the gentle breeze is Me (The Holy Spirit) supporting you, leading you. The string wrapped around the branches are like the trials & difficulties of life. I am there to get you through these, to guide and support you.

BUT

You have to do your part!
You need to untangle the strings, and then I will lift you up, higher. Every string unravelled from a branch means the kite will soar higher and higher.

As you reach new heights, you will see things so much clearer, in a new way.

You will be able to see the world, but not be "of it".

Scriptures:

"But those who wait for the Lord (who expect, look for and hope in Him) shall change & renew their strength & power; they shall lift their wings and mount up (close to God) as eagles (mount up to the sun); they shall run and not be weary, they shall walk and not faint or become tired."

Isaiah 40:31

"And set your minds and keep them set on what is above (the higher things) not on the things that are on the earth."

Colossians 3:2

"But you are not living the life of the flesh, you are living the life of the Spirit, if the (Holy) Spirit of God (really) dwells within you (directs and controls you)."

Romans 8:9

"For the love of Christ controls and urges and impels us, because we are of the opinion and conviction that (if) One died for all, then all died; And He died for all, so that all those who live might live no longer to and for themselves, but to and for Him Who died and was raised again for their sake."

2 Corinthians 5:14

"And (so that you can know and understand) what is the immeasurable and unlimited and surpassing greatness of His power in and for us who believe, as demonstrated in the working of His mighty strength."

Ephesians 1:19

Is there anything God may be asking you to unravel? To change in some way? To look at a relationship in another way perhaps? Or something else?

…..

…..

…..

…..

…..

…..

…..

…..

…..

…..

"I have perseverance, character and hope..." Rom 5:3-4

Like walking in the snow,
He covers our dirty footprints

God uses so many ways to speak to us.

Big plump fluffy snowflakes were falling, fluttering silently, making a soft carpet of white, and dulling down the worldly sounds.

As I looked through my lounge window at the snow, He used the wonderful scenery to get my attention.

Just watch how the gentle flurry of flakes cover things so beautifully. Walking in the snow, whilst it is snowing, is like your walk with Jesus.

Every time you take a step in the snow, the flakes settle and the footprints disappear.

That's just what Jesus does isn't it?

He gives you fresh snow to walk in every day, and covers your dirty footprints that you leave behind!

I am so thankful that He does!

Scriptures:

"Above all things, have intense and unfailing love for one another, for love covers a multitude of sins (forgives and disregards the offences of others)."

1 Peter 4:8

"But if we (really) are living and walking in the Light, as He (Himself) is in the Light, we have (true, unbroken) fellowship with one another, and the blood of Jesus Christ His Son cleanses (removes) us from all sin and guilt (keeps us cleansed from sin in all its forms and manifestations)."

1 John 1:7

"Blessed and happy and to be envied are those whose iniquities are forgiven and whose sins are covered up and completely buried. Blessed and happy and to be envied is the person of whose sin the Lord will take no account nor reckon it against him."

Romans 4:7-8

"But let all those who take refuge and put their trust in You rejoice, let them ever sing and shout for joy, because You make a covering over them and defend them; let those who also love Your name be joyful in You and be in high spirits."

Psalm 5:11

"Hatred stirs up contentions, but love covers all transgressions."

Proverbs 10:12

Is there anything you would like to ask Father forgiveness for? Anything you want covered by His grace?

…..

…..

…..

…..

…..

…..

…..

…..

…..

…..

"I am not under law, but under grace" Rom 6:14

<u>Release that protective grip on your heart,</u>
<u>let it be free</u>

Jesus paid for us to be free!

This includes every part of our being and every part of our lives.

He made me realise I had been clasping my heart tightly in my hand.
I thought I was protecting it from being hurt again, but all I was doing was squishing the life out of it.

Jesus showed me what I had to do.

Open my hand , and set my heart free.

My heart was then

free to love,
free to trust,
free to hope,
free to forgive,
free to live!

Scriptures:

"And you will know the Truth, and the Truth will set you free."

John 8:32

"Because of and through the heart of tender mercy and loving kindness of our God, a Light from on high, will dawn upon us and visit (us)."

Luke 1:78

"By having the eyes of your heart flooded with light, so that you can know and understand the hope to which He has called you, and how rich is His glorious inheritance in the saints (His set apart ones)."

Ephesians 1:18

"Comfort and encourage your hearts and strengthen them (make them steadfast and keep them unswerving) in every good work and word."

2 Thessalonians 2:17

"Trust in, lean on, rely on, and have confidence in Him at all times, you people; pour out your hearts before Him. God is a refuge for us (a fortress and a high tower)."

Psalm 62:8

Are you holding any hurt in your heart that needs to be set free? Do yourself a favour and let it go!

…..

…..

…..

…..

…..

…..

…..

…..

…..

…..

…..

"I have now no condemnation." Rom 8:1

Don't struggle in the dark,
let Him show you the Light

In a dream, which seemed more like a nightmare until God enlightened me, I was quietly sitting at the back of a church.

Suddenly from behind, someone threw a sack right over me. It was thrust violently down to my waist. It felt like two or more people were holding me down. I lashed out, kicking and trying to move my arms to grab at the cloth sack desperately.

The darkness was terrifying, not knowing what was happening and so fearful of what these people were planning.

It seemed I was fighting for ages, when, unexpectedly the sack was gently and swiftly lifted off me and I was in the light.

Safe. Secure.
We can battle in our own strengths, staying in the dark
or
ask Father for help.

Lean on Him and
He will bring us Light and hope,
gently and swiftly!

Scriptures:

"The people who sat (dwelt enveloped) in darkness have seen a great Light, and for those who sat in the land and shadow of death, Light has dawned."

Matthew 4:16

"To shine upon and give Light to those who sit in darkness and in the shadow of death, to direct and guide our feet in a straight line into the way of peace."

Luke 1:79

"In Him was life, and the Life was the Light of men."   John 1:4

"Once more Jesus addressed the crowd. He said, I am the Light of the world. He who follows Me will not be walking in the dark, but will have the Light which is Life."

John 8:12

"And God saw that the light was good (suitable, pleasant) and He approved it; and God separated the light from the darkness."

Genesis 1:4

"For with You is the fountain of life, in Your light do we see light."

Psalm 36:9

"For You have delivered my life from death, yes, and my feet from falling, that I may walk before God in the light of life and of the living."   Psalm 56:13

Is there a problem where you need light to shine on the darkness? To have clarity rather than confusion?

…..

…..

…..

…..

…..

…..

…..

…..

…..

…..,...

…..

…..

"I am full of goodness and filled with all knowledge, as it is given by the Holy Spirit." Rom 15:14

Stop trying so hard, let Him lift the burden

During a time of worship I saw myself in a room, where everything around me was falling to pieces.
My hands were raised,
to hold the ceiling up in a vain attempt to stop it from tumbling down on top of me!

I heard someone enter the room and felt an elbow nudge in my side.
I looked around and there He was!

Jesus!

He had a huge cheeky smile, His face beaming with joy.

As I started to smile back at Him, He raised His arms high and took the weight of the ceiling from my hands.

He had lifted the burden from me!

Thank You Jesus!

Scriptures:

"And (Jesus) said to His disciples, Therefore, I tell you, do not be anxious and troubled (with cares) about your life, as to what you will (have to) eat; or about your body, as to what you will (have to) wear."

Luke 12:22

"Casting the whole of your care (all your anxieties, all your worries, all your concerns, once and for all) on Him, for He cares for you affectionately and cares about you watchfully."

1 Peter 5:7

"But You, O Lord, are a shield for me, my glory, and the lifter of my head."

Psalm 3:3

"We are hedged in (pressed) on every side (troubled and oppressed in every way), but not cramped or crushed; we suffer embarrassments and are perplexed and unable to find a way out, but not driven to despair ."

2 Corinthians 4:8

"But He said to me, My grace (My favour and loving-kindness and mercy) is enough for you (sufficient against any danger and enables you to bear the trouble manfully); for My strength and power are made perfect (fulfilled and completed) and show themselves most effective in (your weakness)."

2 Corinthians 12:9

Are there any anxieties, worries, or burdens you can pass to God today?

…...

…...

…...

…...

…...

…...

…...

…...

…...

…...

…...

"I am not lacking in any spiritual gift." 1 Cor 1:7

Take that bag back,
see how light you feel

My first morning, after receiving Jesus, The Lord asked me to visit someone I needed to forgive!
Not liking confrontation, my heart was in my mouth, as I made my way there.
I had a heavy heart.

However, I seemed to have an inner strength and I was surprised at what I was doing!

I took a deep breath, walked in and forgave.
I did what God had done for me the previous day.
What He does every day for me.

As I left, I felt as though I was walking on air, such was the lightness in my step.

I saw that I had entered the building with an extremely heavy, cumbersome rucksack upon my back.
I'd then dropped the weighty bag at the feet of the person I had forgiven, and left
it there!

I was, now, able to walk upright as I had no weight upon my shoulders.

Forgiveness is to think we are letting the prisoner free, only to discover, that we were the one in
bondage!

Scriptures:

"And even if he sins against you seven times a day, and turns to you seven times and and says, I repent (I am sorry), you must forgive him (give up resentment and consider the offence as recalled and annulled)."

Luke 17:4

"For if you forgive people their trespasses (their reckless and wilful sins, leaving them, letting them go, and giving up resentment) your heavenly Father will also forgive you."

Matthew 6:14

"And whenever you stand praying, if you have anything against anyone, forgive him and let it drop (leave it, let it go), in order that your Father Who is in heaven may also forgive you your (own) failings and shortcomings and let them drop."

Mark 11:25

"The Lord God is a Sun and Shield; the Lord bestows (present) grace and favour and (future) glory (honour, splendour and heavenly bliss)! No good thing will He withhold from those who walk uprightly."

Psalm 84:11

"And become useful and helpful and kind to one another, tender-hearted (compassionate, understanding, loving-hearted), forgiving one another (readily and freely), as God in Christ forgave you." phesians 4:32

You may think you have forgiven everyone you need to, but ask God if there is some thing or some one you may have forgotten?

…..

…..

…..

…..

…..

…..

…..

…..

…..

…..

"I have been given God's spirit so I can understand what God has freely given." 1 Cor 2:12

54

Remove the hook from your heart,
is not letting them 'off the hook'

Forgiveness can be such a difficult act to carry out sometimes, well most of the time if we are honest. We think that when we do, we are letting the person 'off the hook'.

God gave me a powerful image to help me through this issue.

I looked down to find a huge, ugly meat hook plunged and protruding from my heart. The pain, as you can imagine, unbearable, as it was buried so deeply into that delicate part of me. My heart bleeding. Hanging off the other end of the hook was the person I felt I had so much to forgive.

Was that person hurting because of my unforgiveness?
Who knows?
The hook was under the person's trouser belt, unaware that it was even there!

Yet, the person's full weight was dragging heavily on my torn up, ripped apart, damaged heart.

So, take the hook out of your heart, release yourself from the pain of it all.
Praise God!

I did so, and I watched that person slide off into the distance, stopping when the hook caught hold of The Cross.

Scriptures:

"If you forgive anyone anything, I too forgive that one; and what I have forgiven, if I have forgiven anything, has been for your sakes in the presence (and with the approval) of Christ (the Messiah)."

2Corinthians 2:10

"Be gentle and forbearing with one another and, if one has a difference (a grievance or complaint) against another, readily pardoning each other; even as the Lord has (freely) forgiven you, so must you also (forgive)."

Colossians 3:13

"For if you forgive people their trespasses (their reckless and wilful sins, leaving them, letting them go, and giving up resentment), your heavenly Father will also forgive you."

Matthew 6:14

"Judge not (neither pronouncing judgement nor subjecting to censure), and you will not be judged; do not condemn and pronounce guilty, and you will not be condemned and pronounced guilty; acquit and forgive and release (give up resentment, let it drop), and you will be acquitted and forgiven and released."

Luke 6:37

"And forgive us our debts, as we also have forgiven (left, remitted, and let go of the debts, and have given up resentment against) our debtors."

Matthew 6:12

Sometimes, we also need to forgive ourselves for things that have happened in our past. We can often be much harder on ourselves than others. Is there something?

....

....

....

....

....

....

....

....

....

....

"I have received mercy and do not lose heart." 2 Cor 4:1

Take off that old coat,
there's so many new ones to put on

We all struggle with change.

So often we know we need to change but we resist it.

Why?

Fear?

Even though we may know it is for the best, we find it hard to move outside of our comfort zone.

We can feel secure in what we know, despite the fact it may not be bringing us the results we want.

Our Heavenly Father has so much more planned for us.

He suggested to me one day, take off that old coat, there's so many new ones to put on!

Scriptures:

"Now to Him Who, by (in consequence of) the (action of His) power that is at work within us, is able to (carry out His purpose and) do super-abundantly, far over and above all that we (dare) ask or think, (infinitely beyond our highest prayers, desires, thoughts, hopes or dreams)."

Ephesians 3:20

"The Lord shall open to you His good treasury, the heavens, to give the rain of your land in its season and to bless all the work of your hands; and you shall lend to many nations, but you shall not borrow."

Deuteronomy 28:12

"Moses told the people, Fear not; stand still (firm, confident, undismayed) and see the salvation of the Lord which He will work for you today."

Exodus 14:13

"Be strong, courageous and firm; fear not nor be in terror before them, for it is the Lord your God who goes with you. He will not fail you or forsake you."

Deuteronomy 31:6

"It is the Lord Who goes before you; He will (march) with you; He will not fail you or let you go or forsake you; (let there be no cowardice or flinching, but) fear not, neither become broken (in spirit – depressed, dismayed, and unnerved with alarm).

Deuteronomy 31:8

Is there something God is encouraging you to do? Are you being held back? Why?

…..

…..

…..

…..

…..

…..

…..

…..

…..

…..

"I have the Holy Spirit in my body." 2 Cor 4:7

Don't sit alone on that island, get in that boat

During our lives, many of us will find ourselves in a situation where we are alone, afraid, confused, discouraged and upset as we face a problem.

It is possible for us to become depressed with the heavy burden upon us which can make us weak, and tired.

We recoil in our sadness.
We become unable to reach out to others.

Father does not want us to stay alone, because he knows that it will make us weaker and sadder.

He says to get off that island you have marooned yourself upon.

Get in the boat, get away from the loneliness and find people who are out there to help, support, encourage and
love you!

<u>Scriptures</u>:

"But God, Who comforts and encourages and refreshes and cheers the depressed and the sinking, comforted and encouraged refreshed and cheered us..."   2 Corinthians 7:6

"They cried to You and were delivered; they trusted in, leaned on and confidently relied on You, and were not ashamed or confounded or disappointed."   Psalm 22:5

"Fear not, for you shall not be ashamed; neither be confounded and depressed, for you shall not be put to shame."   Isaiah 54:4

"And be not grieved and depressed, for the joy of the Lord is your strength and stronghold."
Nehemiah 8:10

"The thief comes only in order to steal and kill and destroy. I came that they may have and enjoy life, and have it in abundance (to the full, till it overflows)".   John 10:10

"I have strength for all things in Christ who empowers me (I am ready for anything and equal to anything through Him who infuses inner strength into me; I am self-sufficient in Christ's sufficiency).
Philippeans 4:13

"It is the Lord Who goes before you; He will (march) with you; He will not fail you or let you go or forsake you; fear not, neither become broken (in spirit – depressed, dismayed, and unnerved with alarm).   Deuteronomy 31:8

Are you feeling upset, sad or depressed? Ask God to come into your heart and heal you, and guide you to someone who will encourage you.

…..

…..

…..

…..

…..

…..

…..

…..

…..

…..

"My inner man is being renewed day by day." 2 Cor 4:16

Stay calm in the boat,
then jump on to the water

A deadline approached. Daunted. Overwhelmed!

God showed me an image of a boat bobbing along calmly upon a river.
I was in the boat, relaxed and happy, even though at the end of the river was a waterfalls edge awaiting me!

However, be encouraged, it may look scary and dangerous ahead but if you stay leaning on Me, keep your faith, I will keep you protected, safe and peaceful.

The day before the deadline He woke me to show me that the picture had now changed.
The boat was plummeting over the edge and tumbling through the frothy, cascading water.

Thankfully, I had already jumped out of the boat **on** to the water.
Now, I needed to step out into the supernatural (like Peter did) and walk on the water.

I felt that Father was showing me that, in the boat, we are, obviously, 'looked after' by Him. We are in the 'natural' and we pray for Him to do things for us.
On the water, however, the role changes slightly. We now need to really look to Jesus, focus on Him as we walk in the 'supernatural'.
We have to do more for ourselves in order that we can be like Jesus, and do as He did.

Scriptures:

"After He got into the boat, His disciples followed Him.
And suddenly, behold, there arose a violent storm on the sea, so that the boat was covered up by the waves; but He was sleeping.
And they went and awakened Him, saying Lord, rescue and preserve us! We are perishing!
And He said to them, Why are you timid and afraid, O you of little faith? Then He got up and rebuked the winds and the sea, and there was a great and wonderful calm (a perfect peaceableness)."
Matthew 8:23-26

"And in the fourth watch (between 3.00-6.00 a.m.) of the night, Jesus came to them, walking on the sea.
And when the disciples saw Him walking on the sea, they were terrified and said, It is a ghost! And they screamed out with fright.
But instantly He spoke to them, saying, Take courage. I AM! Stop being afraid!
And Peter answered Him, Lord, if it is You, command me to come to You on the water.
He said, Come! So, Peter got out of the boat and walked on the water and he came toward Jesus."
Matthew 14:25-29

"In returning (to Me) and resting (in Me) you shall be saved; in quietness and in (trusting) confidence shall be your strength."   Isaiah 30:15

"I am strong, vigorous and very courageous. I am not afraid, neither am I dismayed, for the Lord my God is with me wherever I go."   Joshua 1:9

Do you need His strength? Do you need some courage to do something new?

....

....

....

....

....

....

....

....

....

....

"I live by faith not by sight." 2 Cor 5:7

Faith is the pipeline, for His blessings to flow

"Without faith we cannot please Him".

I, initially and naively, understood this to mean that if we did not believe in God and His promises, He would be angry with us.

I had completely misunderstood! So sorry Father.

Now, thankfully, I do understand.

God taught me, that if we do not believe that He is able and can do the things that we ask of Him, and keep believing, then He is 'deprived' of the opportunity to work in that situation.

He needs our belief in Him, because when we keep believing that the answer to our prayer will be seen, He is being given permission to keep working in it. We do our part and He is able to do His.

Faith is needed to sustain God's involvement to work all things together for the good.

He showed me that faith is like the pipeline for His blessings to flow through to us.

Scriptures:

"But without faith it is impossible to please and be satisfactory to Him."

Hebrews 11:6

"Do not, therefore, fling away your fearless confidence, for it carries a great and glorious compensation and reward." Hebrews 10:35

"And Jesus, replying, said to them, Have faith in God (constantly)." Mark 11:22

"And he who believes in (has faith in, clings to, relies on) the Son has (now possesses) eternal life.

John 3:36

"Now faith is the assurance (the confirmation, the title deed) of the things (we) hope for, being the proof of things (we) do not see and the conviction of their reality (faith perceiving as a real fact what is not revealed to the senses). Hebrews 11:1

"Then He touched their eyes, saying, According to your faith and trust and reliance (on the power invested in Me) be it done to you;" Matthew 9:29

"And whatever you ask for in prayer, having faith and (really) believing, you will receive."

Matthew 21:22

"And Jesus, replying, said to them, Have faith in God (constantly)."

Mark 11:22

Is there something you are believing God for?

....

....

....

....

....

....

....

....

....

....

....

"I have grace and peace." Eph 1:2

Faith and doubt,
like oil and water

When we have faith, we can move mountains. We can expect miraculous answers to prayer.

When we doubt, we are actually being fearful. We are frightened the prayer may not be answered. As soon as we think this it can stop the flow of faith.

It's like oil and water, God said, they don't mix.

That is a good visual reminder when we are being tossed about from belief to unbelief.

Don't doubt!

God does **not** break His promises.

When we believe, we receive.

He will deliver.

Scriptures:

"Only it must be in faith that he asks with no waivering (no hesitating, no doubting). For the one who waivers (hesitates, doubts) is like the billowing surge out at sea that is blown hither and thither and tossed by the wind."
James 1:6

"Be assured and understand that the trial and proving of your faith bring out endurance and steadfastness and patience."
James 1:3

"At once the father of the boy gave (an eager, piercing, inarticulate) cry with tears, and he said, Lord, I believe! (Constantly) help my weakness of faith."
Luke 8:25

"Preserve my life, for I am godly and dedicated; O my God, save Your servant, for I trust in You (leaning and believing on You, committing all and confidently looking to You, without fear or doubt)."
Psalm 86:2

"She tastes and sees that her gain from work (with and for God) is good; her lamp goes not out, but it burns on continually through the night (of trouble, privation, or sorrow, warning away fear, doubt and distrust)."
Proverbs 31:18

"But that you may know positively and beyond a doubt that the Son of Man has right and authority and power on earth to forgive sins – He said to the paralyzed man."
Mark 2:10

Is your faith waivering whilst waiting for an answer to prayer? Ask Him to help you with your unbelief or patience.

…..

…..

…..

…..

…..

…..

…..

…..

…..

…..

"I have all things under my feet." Eph 1:22

Use your shield of faith,
or just step aside

We all are attacked by the enemy, at different times, and varying intensities.

The events or attacks can seem like fiery arrows flying at us, from all angles sometimes.

We have our spiritual armour to protect us from these (Ephesians 6:10-18), so put up your shield of faith to defend yourself daily.

Although, one day, the Lord encouraged me to also do something that is even easier, if we can remember amidst the conflict.

To just step to one side and watch Him catch the arrow!

He tells us to let Him deal with the problems that are part of our every day life . Unfortunately, it is not an immediate reaction for us to step aside, but it can come with practise!

So, in every situation ask,
"OK then Holy Spirit, what shall I do?"

And listen... And follow!

Scriptures:

"Be strong, vigorous, and very courageous. Be not afraid, neither be dismayed, for the Lord your God is with you wherever you go."   Joshua 1:9

"For by You I can run through a troop, and by my God I can leap over a wall."

Psalm 18:29

"He will cover you with His pinions, and under His wings shall you trust and find refuge; His truth and His faithfulness are a shield and a buckler."   Psalm 91:4

"The Lord causes your enemies who rise up against you to be defeated before your face; they shall come out against you one way and flee before you seven ways."

Deuteronomy 28:7

"Fear not (there is nothing to fear) for I am with you; do not look around in terror and be dismayed, for I am your God. I will strengthen and harden you to difficulties, yes, I will help you; yes, I will hold you up and retain you with My (victorious) right hand of rightness and justice."

Isaiah 41:10

"He makes wars to cease to the end of the earth. He breaks the bow into pieces and snaps the spear in two. He burns the chariots in the fire.
Let be and be still and know (recognise and understand) that I am God."

Psalm 46:9

Have you any battles going on that you need His help with?

…..

…..

…..

…..

…..

…..

…..

…..

…..

…..

"I have a power source within me which is able to do abundantly beyond all that I ask or think."
Eph 3:20

Sword of the Word,
a bit like a blow torch

Putting on our Spiritual Armour every day to protect ourselves from the enemy is so important.

The enemy comes to steal, kill and destroy our faith.
He steals, kills, destroys our joy by feeding us negative thoughts, by using other hurting people,
our circumstances and all sorts of things that are going on in our lives.

Stealing our happiness and strength is a bonus to Satan.
What he desperately craves is our faith.

That is why God has provided us with Spiritual Armour,
to equip us to defend ourselves... to fight back.

God's Words are power!

His Words created the world. His Words, when spoken out, will come to pass.

I had an image.
As we speak Father's Words it's like fire spewing out from our mouths to the powers and principalities
of darkness.
The flames lash out at the enemy and his demons, and they have no option but to recoil and flee!

Scriptures:

"Death and life are in the power of the tongue, and they who indulge in it shall eat the fruit of it (for death or life)."

Proverbs 18:21

"A man has joy in making an apt answer, and a word spoken at the right *moment* – how good it is!"

Proverbs15:23

"Do not let yourself be overcome by evil, but overcome (master) evil with good."

Romans 12:21

"So be subject to God. Resist the devil (stand firm against him) and he will flee from you."

James 4:7

"Put on God's whole armour (the armour of a heavy-armed soldier which God supplies) that you may be able successfully to stand up against (all) the strategies and deceits of the devil."

Ephesians 6:11

"Therefore you shall lay up these My words in your (minds and)hearts and in your (entire) being and bind them for a sign upon your hands and as forehead bands between your eyes. And you shall write them upon the doorposts of your house and on your gates."

Deuteronomy 11:18

Do you need His protection for something in particular? Ask Him to help you.

…..

…..

…..

…...……...

…..

…..

…..

…..

…..

…..

…..

…..

"The peace of God guards my heart and mind as I pray with thanksgiving in the midst of everything."
Phil 2:15

Flick off the flies,
just like the lies of the enemy

The Lord was speaking to me about resisting the lies that the enemy continually speaks to us.

I was walking happily along when suddenly I was bombarded with many flies buzzing around me.

YUCK!

Immediately, my arms were flapping about, swatting madly at the flies to get them off and away.

Jesus spoke to me, explaining that this is exactly how we should react when a "lie" is spoken to us.

Resist it!

When a fly lands on us, our natural, instinctive reaction is to flick it off, because we do not want their disgusting germs that they carry, to settle on us. They carry infection and we don't want that!

That is what the lies of the enemy do isn't it?
If we let them land on us, listen to them, there is a possibility that we may begin to believe them and then our feelings and behaviour becomes affected, infected.

So, flick of the (f)lies of the enemy!

Scriptures:

"But no weapon that is formed against you shall prosper, and every tongue that shall rise against you in judgement you shall show to be in the wrong. This (peace, righteousness, security, triumph over opposition) is the heritage of the servants of the Lord."   Isaiah 54:17

"Who shall bring any charge against God's elect (when it is) God Who justifies (that is, Who puts us in right relation to Himself? Who shall come forward and accuse or impeach those whom God has chosen? Will God, Who acquits us?)"   Romans 8:33-34

"Do not be conformed to this world (this age), (fashioned after and adapted to its external, superficial customs), but be transformed (changed) by the (entire) renewal of your mind."
Romans 12:2

"(In as much as we) refute arguments and theories and reasonings and every proud and lofty thing that sets itself up against the (true) knowledge of God; and we lead every thought and purpose away captive into the obedience of Christ."   2 Corinthians 10:5

"Be well balanced (temperate, sober of mind), be vigilant and cautious at all times; for that enemy of yours, the devil, roams around like a lion roaring (in fierce hunger), seeking someone to seize upon and devour.
Withstand him; be firm in faith (against his onset – rooted, established, strong, immovable and determined), knowing that the same (identical) sufferings are appointed to your brotherhood (the whole body of Christians) throughout the world."   1 Peter 5:8,9

What lies have you been listening to? Ask God to show you the Truth.

…...

…...

…...

…...

…...

…...

…...

…...

…...

…...

"I can do all things through Christ who strengthens me."   Phil 4:13

<u>Chop down those weeds,</u>
<u>so they dont strangle your seeds</u>

When we want our garden to look beautiful we need to put in seeds and young plants, keep them watered and fed.

Unfortunately, weeds seem to be able to grow anywhere and from nowhere! They don't need any nurturing, feeding or watering. Suddenly they appear!

It can happen along our path that we walk too! We may have good intentions, begin spending regular quality time with our Heavenly Father. We start to see beautiful, cultivated growth along our pathway. Then from nowhere weeds are there, pulling, tugging, and strangling the good seeds that have been sown.

So many things can sneak up on us to stop us growing. Our good intentions are swamped by business and distractions.

If we don't get intentional, stay focussed and continue feeding ourselves it will result in the weeds strangling the seeds.

Focus on the flowers!

Scriptures:

"I love those who love Me, and those who seek Me early and diligently shall find Me."

Proverbs 8:17

"He becomes poor who works with a slack and idle hand, but the hand of the diligent makes rich."

Proverbs 10:4

"For He is our God and we are the people of His pasture and the sheep of His hand. Today if you will hear His voice,
harden not your hearts."

Psalm 95:7, 8

"While anyone is hearing the Word of the kingdom and does not grasp and comprehend it, the evil one comes and snatches away what was sown in his heart. This is what was sown along the roadside." As for what was sown on good soil, this is he who hears the Word and grasps and comprehends it; he indeed bears fruit and yields in one case a hundred times as much as was sown, in another sixty times as much, and in another thirty."

Matthew 13:19, 23

"The poor and afflicted shall eat and be satisfied; they shall praise the Lord – they who (diligently) seek for, inquire of, and for Him and require Him (as their greatest need). May your hearts be quickened now and forever!"

Psalm 22:26

Ask God to guide you in His word, to help you keep your focus. Maybe ask Him for a particular scripture!

…..

…..

…..

…..

…..

…..

…..

…..

…..

…..

"In Christ I have been made complete." Col 2:10

Step over the guard dog,
he's stopping you from entering through
the door to your destiny

God has a plan for each and every one of us. He has given each of us the gifts and talents to achieve this.

Most of us struggle to believe we have what it takes. And when we do get to that stage of believing, we find it hard to claim it.

What stops us? Fear!

We want to walk in His plans but it usually means we will need to step out of our comfort zone.

Those that are achieving the dream have felt the fear but chosen to do it anyway!

God declares - "Fear not".
With faith, fear will not win, because faith is mightier than fear.

So, step over that ferocious guard dog that is stopping you from walking through the door to your destiny.
Actually, he may not really be that scary!

Scriptures:

"Fear not, nor be dismayed; be strong and of good courage."

Joshua 10:25

"Yes, though I walk through the (deep, sunless) valley of the shadow of death, I will fear or dread no evil, for You are with me; Your rod (to protect) and Your staff (to guide), they comfort me."

Psalm 23:4

"The Lord is my Light and my Salvation – whom shall I fear or dread? The Lord is the refuge and stronghold of my life – of whom shall I be afraid?"

Psalm 27:1

"The fear of man brings a snare, but whoever leans on, trusts in, and puts his confidence in the Lord is safe and set on high."   Proverbs 29:25

"Do not be seized with alarm and struck with fear, little flock, for it is your Father's good pleasure to give you the kingdom!"

Luke 12:32

"For God did not give us a spirit of fear and timidity (of cowardice, of craven and cringing and fawning fear), but (He has given us a spirit) of power and of love and of calm and well-balanced mind and discipline and self-control."

2 Timothy 1:7

Do you know what His plans are for you? What special gifts has He blessed you with? Ask Him.

…..

…..

…..

…..

…..

…..

…..

…..

…..

…..

…..

"The faithful Lord will strengthen and protect me from the evil one." 2 Thess 3:3

<u>Heart strings,</u>
<u>our hearts are connected to Fathers</u>

Two heart shaped balloons
tied to each other.

When one balloon is pulled,
the other will also feel the effect and
be moved.

Just like our heart is connected to
Father's.

When someone hurts us and pulls at
our heart strings,
Father feels it too!

That's what He showed me!

Scriptures:

"He who dwells in the secret place of the Most High shall remain stable and fixed under the shadow of the Almighty (Whose power no foe can withstand)."

Psalm 91:1

"Fear not (there is nothing to fear), for I am with you; do not look around you in terror and be dismayed, for I am your God. I will strengthen and harden you to difficulties, yes I will help you; yes, I will hold you up and retain you with My (victorious) right hand of rightness and justice."

Isaiah 41:10

"O Give thanks to the Lord, for He is good; for His mercy and loving kindness endure forever."

Psalm 118:1

"Bless (affectionately, gratefully praise) the Lord, O my soul, and forget not (one of) all His benefits - Who forgives (every one of) all your iniquities, Who heals (each one of) all your diseases."

Psalm 103:2, 3

"But certainly God has heard me, He has given heed to the voice of my prayer. Blessed be God, Who has not rejected my prayer nor removed His mercy and loving-kindness from being (as it always is) with me.

Psalm 66:19, 20

Has something tugged at your heartstrings lately? He understands how you are feeling. Chat to Him about it.

…..

…..

…..

…..

…..

…..

…..

…..

…..

…..

"For God has not given me a spirit of fear, but of power and love and a sound mind." 2 Tim 1:7

Stand under the waterfall,
and get soaked

Sometimes we can be bewildered at what goes on around us in the world. It can leave us feeling confused.

At such a time in my life the Lord presented me with a beautiful waterfall, cascading noisily in the warm sunlight.

Standing under the fall of that water is like being under My Grace.

You can be soaked in My love, mercy and favour.
You can still look out from the waterfall and see the world, good and bad.

You could step out from what is falling upon you and still see the same things,
but, you will not be getting soaked with My love, My mercy,
My favour, and My grace.

When bad things happen, some choose to blame God, and sadly, give up on Him.

Please remember, God is good all the time.

The waterfall flows continuously – get under it, get soaked, and keep soaking yourself in Him.

Scriptures:

"We are assured and know that (God being a partner in their labour) all things work together and are (fitting into a plan) for good to and for those who love God and are called according to (His) design and purpose."

Romans 8:28

"But He said to me, My grace (My favour and loving-kindness and mercy) is enough for you (sufficient against any danger and enables you to bear the trouble manfully); for My strength and power are made perfect (fulfilled and completed) and show themselves most effective in (your) weakness."

2 Corinthians 12:9

"Yet amid all these things we are more than conquerors and gain a surpassing victory through Him Who loved us.
For I am persuaded beyond doubt (am sure) that neither death nor life, nor angels nor principalities, nor things impending and threatening nor things to come, nor powers,
Nor height nor depth, nor anything else in all creation will be able to separate us from the love of God which is in Christ Jesus our Lord."

Romans 8:37-39

"So we take comfort and are encouraged and confidently and boldly say, The Lord is my Helper; I will not be seized with alarm (I will not fear or dread or be terrified). What can man can do to me?"

Hebrews 13:6

Are you being challenged by something that has happened to you, or a loved one? Ask God to comfort and guide you.

…..…..

…..

…..

…..

…..

…..

…..

…..

…..

…..

…..

…..

"I have entered into His rest." Heb 4:3

The tree next to the stream, grows more fruit and better fruit

I was struggling with some tough emotions and circumstances, so as I walked my dog, I asked Father to give me a picture to encourage me, to know that He was with me.

I looked across at some trees in the field and He spoke.

One tree next to a stream, a few others further away.

The tree next to the stream has more fruit... the best fruit.

Like His Living Water, if you use it, keep close to it, don't wander off, you will be more fruitful.

Then, you will be a good witness for Jesus because your fruit will be better than those who do not know Him!

So, don't get discouraged, others will see the differences in you.

Lets aim to make the best fruit – for
His Glory!

Scriptures:

"But if from there you will seek (inquire for and require as necessity) the Lord your God, you will find Him if you (truly) seek Him with all your heart (and mind) and soul and life."

Deuteronomy 4:29

"For skilful and godly Wisdom is better than rubies or pearls, and all the things that may be desired are not to be compared to it."

Proverbs 8:11

"Jesus replied, I am the Bread of Life. He who comes to Me will never be hungry, and he who believes in and cleaves to and trusts in and relies on Me will never thirst any more (at any time)."

John 6:35

"(Most) blessed is the man who believes in, trusts in, and relies on the Lord, and whose hope and confidence, the Lord is.
For he shall be like a tree planted by the waters that spreads out its roots by the river; and it shall not see and fear when heat comes; but its leaf shall be green. It shall not be anxious and full of care in the year of drought, nor shall it cease yielding fruit."

Jeremiah 17:7,8

"Take heed to yourselves, lest your (minds and) heartstrings be deceived and you turn aside and serve other gods and worship them."

Deuteronomy 11:16

How can you bear more fruit?

…..

…..

…..

…..

…..

…..

…..

…..

…..

…..

"God generously and without reproach gives to me wisdom if I ask Him." James 1:5

<u>The Rock, on which I stand</u>

After God rescued me from an emotional situation, that dragged me down into very dark waters for a few days, I thanked Him and began to write...

The Rock is always here!
I stand on my Rock.
Waves lash at my feet, so what! Waves wash up to my waist.
I do not slip off my Rock, my feet are steady.
Waves fierce, ferocious engulf me. I do slip, I lose my footing.
Suddenly, I am in the thrashing waves.
Like arms cruelly grabbing at me, dragging me down and under.
I am drowning! Nevertheless.....God!
He reaches down to me, because He loves me.
He subdues the waves, because He is all powerful and can change circumstances.
He lifts me up, because He comforts me.
I climb back up onto my Rock.
Because I wait on the Lord, He changes and renews my strength and power.
He lifts my wings to mount up like eagles, as I stand back upon my Rock.

Praise God!
You are my Rock.
You are always here.
Thank You so much.

Scriptures:

"So everyone who hears these words of Mine and acts upon them (obeying them) will be like a sensible (prudent, practical, wise) man who built his house upon the rock.
And the rain fell and the floods came and the winds blew and beat against that house, yet it did not fall, because it had been founded on the rock."   Matthew 7:24, 25

"The Lord is my Rock, my Fortress, and my Deliverer, my God, my keen and firm Strength in Whom I will trust and take refuge, my Shield, and the Horn of my salvation, my High Tower.
I will call upon the Lord, Who is to be praised, so shall I be saved from my enemies."
Psalm 18:2, 3

"The fear of man brings a snare, but whoever leans on, trusts in, and puts his confidence in the Lord is safe and set on high."   Proverbs 29 :25

"Because he has set his love upon Me, therefore, will I deliver him; I will set him on high, because he knows and understands My name (has a personal knowledge of My mercy, love, and kindness – trusts and relies on Me, knowing I will never forsake him, no, never).
He shall call upon Me, and I will answer him; I will be with him and honour him.
With long life will I satisfy him and show him My salvation."
Psalm 91:14-16

"He is the Rock, His work is perfect, for all His ways are law and justice. A God of faithfulness without breach or deviation, just and right is He."   Deuteronomy 32:4

God is faithful. He NEVER breaks a promise. Every word in His book are promises to you. What promise are you believing for?

…..

…..

…..

…..

…..

…..

…..

…..

…..

…..

"Because I keep His commandments and do the things that are pleasing to His sight, whatever I ask I receive from Him." 1 John 3:22

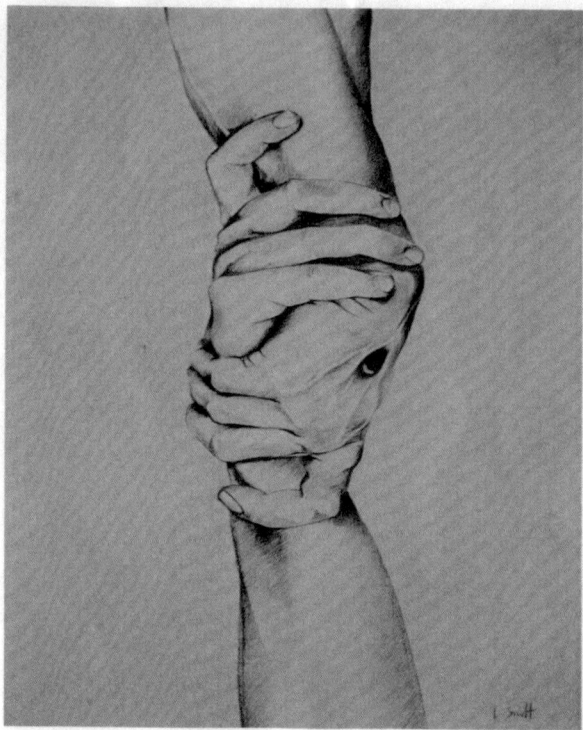

If you reach out
Jesus can grab hold of you

If you have not yet asked Jesus into your life and would like to have a relationship with Him, here is a simple prayer, to invite Him in.

Lord Jesus Christ,
I am sorry for the things I have done wrong in my life.
Please forgive me.
I now turn from everything which I know is wrong.
Thank you that you died on the cross for me so that I could be forgiven and set free.
Thank you that you offer me forgiveness and the gift of your Spirit. I now receive that gift.
Please come into my life by your Holy Spirit, to be with me forever.
Thank you Lord Jesus. Amen.

If you have sincerely prayed, believing in your heart the words you said, you are now part of God's family, you have eternal life, and you are filled with the Holy Spirit. Congratulations! A new life in Jesus!

It is **so** important to find people who can support, guide and encourage you along this exciting journey. Although we have the Holy Spirit to lead us, we still need each other. Find a Spirit filled church to enable you to grow. To help you learn who you now are and what you now have, because of who Jesus is and all that He has done for you.
For everyone!

Some recommended reading

Since receiving Jesus as my Lord and Saviour, I have read many books. I have never read so much in my life. I love it! They can help to bring you amazing understanding, and improve your walk along your exciting new journey. There are, of course, differing views of scripture. It is sad that Father's family interpret His Word in such a wide diverse way. I say sad, because Father desires unity. For united we stand, and divided we fall. We are human though, and imperfect, which is why we all need Him. So, we must try to be respectful of the differences in denominations, and desire always to seek His Truth and to love one another. When we need to seek answers to questions raised by books and teachings, we are blessed to have The Counsellor and His Word. We should always return to the scriptures and ask The Holy Spirit to bring revelation to us. Here are a few that will encourage you:

The Secret Power of speaking God's Word by Joyce Meyer
Battlefield of the Mind by Joyce Meyer
Power Thoughts by Joyce Meyer
It's Your Time by Joel Osteen
Become a Better You by Joel Osteen
Your Words Hold a Miracle by Joel & John Osteen
Smith Wigglesworth on Healing by Smith Wigglesworth
Psalm 91 – God's Shield of Protection by Peggy Joyce Ruth & Angelia Ruth Schum
The Blood and The Glory by Billye Brim
The Essential Guide to Healing by Bill Johnson & Randy Clark
Forgotten God by Francis Chan
Crazy Love by Francis Chan
Dream by Cesar Castellanos D

Below are a list of websites to explore. These sites have so much to offer, including many free teachings to watch and download, as well as incredible resources available.

Www.lifespringchurch.org.uk (my church!)   www.joycemeyer.org   www.joelosteen.com
www.ibethel.org   www.billwinston.org   www.kcm.org
www.creflodollarministries.org   www.awme.net   www.wisdomministries.org